AT THE CUTTING EDGE

Contemporary Hawaiian Quilting

Linda Arthur, PhD

ISLAND HERITAGE

Published and distributed by

 ISLAND HERITAGE
P U B L I S H I N G

94-411 KŌ'AKI STREET, WAIPAHU, HAWAI'I 96797
Orders: (800) 468-2800 • Information: (808) 564-8800
Fax: (808) 564-8877
www.islandheritage.com

ISBN# : 0-89610-373-0

Second Edition, Fourth Printing - 2005

Book Layout by Angela Wu Ki
Edited by Dianna Grundhauser and Mary Cesar

contents

At the cutting edge:
Contemporary Hawaiian Quilting

Hawaiian quilts are a stunning visual testament to the collision of the Western and Polynesian worlds in the nineteenth century. In 1820 the first permanent residents from the Western world came to Hawai'i to stay and set in motion a chain of events that have repercussions even today. These quilts directly reflect the natural world of the Islands, and the culture of the varied peoples who have inhabited the Hawaiian archipelago. Hawai'i's textiles, more than those of any other region, are intimately tied to their environment and to the breathtaking beauty of the Islands.

All year 'round, Hawai'i is filled with intense colors from the tropical plants that cover the islands. Most people have been thrilled by the wonderful climate and the riot of color found in the flowering trees and other vegetation of Hawai'i. Mark Twain wrote: "It is paradise...the green tone of a forest washes over the edges of a broad bar of orange trees that embrace the mountain like a belt. ...You will note the kinds and colors of all the vegetation, just with a glance of the eye."[1] Mark Twain was just one of the many celebrated visitors who referred to Hawai'i as a paradise. This dramatic colorful landscape has been the source of inspiration for Hawaiian quilts. A few years after Twain's visit, Lucy Isabella Bird came to visit the Hawaiian Islands in 1873 and wrote:

---

1 Mark Twain, *New York Tribune*. Reprinted in *Paradise of the Pacific*, V. 75, January 1963, 13-15. (First published 1893).

2 A soft fiber from the *hāpu'u* tree fern, *pulu* was used for mattress stuffing in nineteenth century Hawai'i.

3 Isabella L. Bird, *Six Months in the Sandwich Islands*. 1873 (1881). (New York: GP Putnam and Sons).

PICTORIAL CONTEMPORARY QUILT
THE QUILTMAKER / Kathy Bento
Design inspired by the painting "The Quiltmaker" by Mary Beckman, and Kumiko Sudo's "Fantasies and Flowers." Ulu pattern by Mary's Treasures. Appliqué and machine quilting by Kathy Bento. 59"x63"

I was delighted to see a four-post bed, with mosquito bars, and a clean *pulu*[2] mattress, with a linen sheet over it, covered with a beautiful quilt with a quaint arabesque pattern on a white ground running round it, and a wreath of green leaves in the center. The native women exercise the utmost ingenuity in the patterns and colours of these quilts. Some of them are quite works of art.[3]

It is clear that by 1873, Hawaiian quilting had already developed into a particular style that was recognizably different from quilting done in the Western world. From traditional roots and materials, Hawaiian quilting has developed into two distinctly different styles; from traditional Hawaiian quilting has come a contemporary art form that adheres to traditional concepts while it simultaneously expands the genre. This consistent pattern found in traditional Hawaiian quilting developed as a result of a uniform set of practices, procedures and *kapu* (taboos) taught within the *'ohana* (family). However, in the past 20 years a recognizably new form of Hawaiian quilting has arisen. Referred to as contemporary Hawaiian quilting, this art form includes a very wide range of styles and techniques. It pushes the bounds; contemporary Hawaiian quilting is now at the cutting edge.

The result of five years of research conducted on the major islands of the state of Hawai'i, this book will briefly present the development of Hawaiian quilting into a traditional art form, followed by an investigation into the evolution of contemporary Hawaiian quilting. In the process, I will provide explanations as to why and how the shift from traditional to contemporary Hawaiian quilting took place.[4]

Quilt designs incorporate and reflect personal expressions of beauty, memories shared and recorded, and events commemorated and preserved. To appreciate the Hawaiian quilt, it is necessary to first investigate the incorporation of Western textiles into Hawai'i. From that, we can understand the evolution of aloha attire and Hawaiian quilting, where we see the interrelationship between the physical and cultural environments.

---

4 Research involved a review of the literature, examination of both traditional and contemporary Hawaiian quilts, and questionnaires sent to quilters on O'ahu, Maui, Hawai'i, Kaua'i, and Moloka'i. Fifty quilters were interviewed in depth, and their comments are presented here as quotes.

QUASI-TRADITIONAL CONTEMPORARY QUILT
PINEAPPLE SUSHI / *Lisa Louise Adams*
Design, appliqué and hand quilting by Lisa
Louise Adams. 54"x56"

A BIT OF HISTORICAL BACKGROUND

The Hawaiian Islands are the most remote group of islands in the world, and are 2,500 miles from the U.S. Mainland. Before human habitation of the Islands, Hawai'i's extreme isolation and lush tropical climate helped to create a unique natural world full of colorful trees and flowers, some of which are found nowhere else on earth. Similarly, this remote location fostered cultural isolation as well. The Hawaiian Islands, the last to be colonized by Polynesians, were settled around 400 AD by people from the Marquesas Islands (2,400 miles away). Polynesian plants and culture arrived on fertile soil when the Marquesans relocated to Hawai'i. For the next 1,300 years, the Hawaiian Islands were unknown to both the Western and Asian worlds. [5] During this time, a rich Hawaiian culture evolved.

The Hawaiians clearly possessed sewing skills prior to any outside contact as evidenced by the tradition of making *kapa* (bark cloth) that originated with the arrival of the Polynesians between A.D. 500 and 800. Layers of kapa were often sewn together and decorated, and the finished bark cloth was used for clothing and bedding. [6] *Kapa*, a cloth made by felting fibers from the inner bark of the paper mulberry tree, was used extensively before Western textiles arrived in the islands. [7]

5 Peter Buck (Te Rangi Hiroa), *Arts and Crafts of Hawai'i*.
   (Honolulu: Bishop Museum Press, 1964).

6 Elizabeth A. Akana, *Hawaiian Quilting: A Fine Art* .
   (Honolulu: Hawaiian Mission Children's Society, 1981), 43.

7 Adrienne L. Kaeppler, *The Fabrics of Hawai'i*. (London:
   F. Lewis Publishers, 1975), 8.

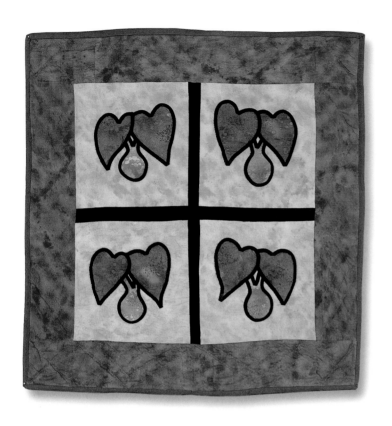

Prior to Western contact, Hawaiian men wore a loincloth called the *malo*, and might also be covered by a cape called a *kīhei*. Women wore the *pā'ū*, a wrapped garment of *kapa* that often had applied geometric designs. The *pā'ū* was worn in several layers.[8] For ritual occasions, Hawaiian royalty wore splendid red and yellow feather capes and cloaks that were avidly collected by visiting seamen.[9]

In addition to clothing, *kapa* was used for bedding (*kapa moe*), and other utilitarian and ceremonial purposes before the missionaries arrived. *Kapa moe* was made of sheets of *kapa* sewn together. Hawaiian *kapa* designs were more refined than Polynesian *tapa*. Most *kapa* was made from the inner bark of the *wauke* (paper mulberry) plant. Women used wooden mallets to pound the strips of bark together to form sheets of various sizes, textures, and thickness, and finally *kapa* was colored by native dyes and decorated with block printing, a technique not found elsewhere in Polynesia.[10]

With the discovery of the Hawaiian Islands by Captain James Cook in 1778 and the subsequent arrival of explorers, merchants, whalers, and missionaries from the Western world, native Hawaiians developed new techniques and designs. They eagerly examined and then creatively adapted Western designs. Woven fabric was introduced during this time as calicoes, chintzes, and silks (from China), and increasingly became available through the trade of Hawaiian sandalwood to seafaring merchants from Asia and the West. Decorations on *kapa* began to imitate the patterns of these imported fabrics. Rapidly, traditional Hawaiian culture subsumed many of the foreign elements. Hawaiian craftsmen found that newly introduced metal tools could easily be adapted to traditional techniques. As a result, designs and motifs found in the material culture of Hawaiians soon became increasingly detailed.[11]

Permanent residents from the Western world, American missionaries, arrived in Hawai'i in 1820. Prior to that time, the indigenous Hawaiians primarily had contact with outsiders through the sandalwood trade. This was a lucrative business for the Hawaiians, and *ali'i* (royalty) were able to live in splendor befitting their station in life.

Although it is not certain when the transition from decorated bark cloth bedding to quilted fabric bedcovers occurred, the visual similarity between the designs on bark cloth and the extant quilts is quite unmistakable. Although the missionaries can be credited with teaching new concepts and techniques in quilt making, the development of the Hawaiian appliqué quilts lies with the Hawaiians themselves, as many of the designs and methods used are found only in Hawai'i.[12]

Top to Bottom (L-R):
APPLIQUÉD AND PIECED CONTEMPORARY QUILT
KALO HANALEI / CYNTHIA HALASEY
Design, appliqué and hand quilting by Cynthia Halasey. 36"x36"

QUASI-TRADITIONAL CONTEMPORARY QUILT
MALAMALAMA / MARY HAUNANI CESAR
Design, appliqué and hand quilting by Mary Cesar. Hand dyed fabric by Marit Kucera. 22"x22"

PIECED CONTEMPORARY QUILT
GRACEFUL PALMS / LINDA LEWIS
Painted and hand quilted by Linda Lewis. 16"x16"

UNUSUAL APPLIQUÉ CONTEMPORARY QUILT
VOLCANO / JOAN McDONALD
Appliqué, embellishment and quilting by Joan McDonald. 24"x21"

8 Linda Arthur, *Aloha Attire: Hawaiian Dress in the Twentieth Century*. (Atglen, PA. Schiffer Publications, 2000).
9 Otto von Kotzebue, *Voyage Around the World*. (London: J. Lindon, 1829).
10 Buck, 1964.
11 Lee Wild, introduction to Reiko Brandon's *The Hawaiian Quilt*. (Honolulu: Honolulu Academy of Arts. 1989).
12 Elizabeth A. Akana, *Hawaiian Quilting*, 1981.

QUASI-TRADITIONAL CONTEMPORARY QUILT
Forever Remembered / Joan Davis
*Design, hand appliqué and hand quilting
by Joan Davis. 90"x90"*

ORIGIN OF HAWAIIAN QUILTING

To date, no one has been able to find definitive proof of the initial development of Hawaiian appliqué quilting. We do know that the patchwork quilts and their construction were introduced to Hawaiians by the wives of American missionaries. The first missionary women arrived in 1820, and were warmly welcomed by some of the highest-ranking Hawaiian men and women. Lucy Thurston, the wife of one of the first missionaries, recorded in her journal:

> Monday morning, April 3rd [1820], the first sewing circle was formed that the sun ever looked down upon in this Hawaiian realm. Kalakua, queen-dowager was directress. She requested all the seven white ladies to take seats with them on mats, on the deck of the *Thaddeus*. Mrs. Holman and Mrs. Ruggles were executive officers to ply the scissors and prepare the work. ...The four native women of distinction were furnished with calico patchwork to sew - a new employment to them. [13]

Soon thereafter, regular supplies of fabric arrived from America. [14] The missionary wives began teaching sewing and other domestic arts to the Hawaiians in 1830. In the course of time, Western cloth, fashions, and quilts were integrated into native ways, the making of *kapa* began to decline, and by the end of the nineteenth century, *kapa* production waned. [15]

While American seamstresses had fabric scraps left over after cutting out their garments, the construction of Hawaiian garments such as *holokū* and *mu'umu'u* at that time left few scraps of fabric. To the Hawaiian seamstresses, it probably seemed illogical to cut new materials into small pieces only to be sewn together to make a patchwork quilt. It was quite natural, therefore, that the Hawaiian women would move toward individual designs. They were accustomed to producing original designs with their own *kapa* beater and wood-blocks from which they made *kapa* designs of their own. [16]

13 Lucy Thurston, 1882.

14 M. T. Dibble, [Typescript letter to her sister]. September 1, 1833; Maria Chamberlain to James Patton, September 25, 1820. Available from Hawaiian Mission Children's Society Library, Mission Houses Museum, Honolulu, HI.

15 Wild, 1989.

16 Stella M. Jones, *Hawaiian Quilts*. (Honolulu: Honolulu Academy of Arts, 1973).

APPLIQUÉD AND PIECED CONTEMPORARY QUILT
Touch of Hawai'i / Chris Piper
Design created by Chris in a workshop taught by
Caryl Bryer Fallert. Machine pieced and
machine quilted by Chris Piper. 24"x36"

It is clear the missionary wives taught patchwork to the Hawaiian women, but it is not known exactly when, or even how the appliquéd Hawaiian quilt evolved. What is most striking about the Hawaiian quilt is the appliqué technique in which a large sheet of fabric is folded again and again, cut into a design, then stitched onto a contrasting background, followed by contour quilting around the motif. Both in technique and style, Hawaiian appliqué reminds us of paper snowflakes made by schoolchildren, a contemporary remnant of cut paper work that was popular in the northeastern United States during the early decades of the nineteenth century. Many Pennsylvania Germans practiced *scherenschnitte*, a form of decorative folded paper cutting. Similar cut paper designs were executed by New England schoolgirls, who crafted pictures with their scissors.

Although no documentary evidence has been found to confirm the theory, paper cutting may have been introduced to Hawai'i by missionary women who came from New England. These designs were produced by cutting multiple layers of folded materials to produce a symmetrical design, and like Hawaiian appliqués, the designs of cut paper pieces were most often based on floral forms. According to Althea Serrao, Hawaiian quilting became a significant form of self-expression during the period of rapid Westernization in the nineteenth century. They had lost their religion, their language and traditions, but sought to retain artistic expression in the quilts. "Every stitch had a meaning and every part of the design had a purpose."[17]

The quilts from America that most closely approximate Hawaiian quilts are Pennsylvania Dutch in origin. These quilts often consist of a central medallion appliqué that resembles the Hawaiian technique, or repeats the same floral design in four large blocks. The Honolulu Academy of Arts has a *scherenschnitte* quilt in their collection, made between 1860-1870, which lends some credibility to the idea that this style of quilt was known in the Islands by the late nineteenth century.[18] However, all theories regarding the origin of the Hawaiian appliquéd quilt are conjecture at this point.

17 Poakalani Serrao, *The Hawaiian Quilt: A Spiritual Experience*. (Mutual Publishing: Honolulu, HI, 1997). 9-10.

18 Robert Shaw, *Hawaiian Quilt Masterpieces*, Hugh Lauter Levin Associates, Inc. 1996.

Top to Bottom (L-R):
ASYMMETRICAL CONTEMPORARY QUILT
No Shoes / Jeni Hardy
Design inspired by Caryl Bryer Fallert
workshop. Appliqué and machine quilting by
Jeni Hardy. Commercial pattern available from
Jeni Hardy. 20"x20"

ASYMMETRICAL CONTEMPORARY QUILT
Bird in Paradise / Linda Spencer
Pattern by EA of Hawaii. Hand appliqué and
hand quilting by Linda Spencer. 20"x22"

QUASI-TRADITIONAL CONTEMPORARY QUILT
Road to Hana / Dianna Grundhauser
Design, appliqué and hand quilting by Dianna
Grundhauser. 45"x45"

QUASI-TRADITIONAL CONTEMPORARY QUILT
African Tulips / Patricia
Lei Murray
Design, hand appliqué
and hand quilting by
Patricia Lei Murray.
47"x47"

A great deal of historical research will be required to definitively determine the origin of this technique. It may be safe to say that the Hawaiian appliqué quilt probably represents the Hawaiian modification of Western appliqué quilts. There are indications that the aura of prestige and wealth associated with the less common Western appliqué quilt may have influenced the Hawaiians in their selection of a quilt style to emulate. Although the methods of cutting an overall design from a single piece of fabric is unique to Polynesia, the Hawaiians may have developed their technique after seeing small Western appliqué designs created in a similar manner. [19] Perhaps we shall never know exactly how or when this distinctive art form originated. Hawaiian quilts nevertheless resulted from the successful integration of styles and techniques from diverse cultures.

In nineteenth century Hawai'i, bright solid color was usually chosen for the appliquéd design and sheeting was used for the background. In the early 1800s, turkey red was the most common Western trade fabric available in Hawai'i and many early quilts incorporated a red-on-white color scheme. New fabrics such as chintzes, calicoes, and dotted swiss, were incorporated into this evolving folk art form. Calico is sometimes seen in the older quilts. The calico was lining cloth from England, and when the Hawaiians saw the English ships docking near Towpath Road (now the *makai* [ocean] end of Richards Street) in Honolulu, they would rush down to buy bolts of the fabric. They would put their hands on their chosen bolt, saying "*paupauaho*," which meant "all out of breath" in Hawaiian. The fabric was given this name. [20]

Prior to quilt construction, fabrics were washed to ensure fastness of color. In early times, this task often was relegated to children who took the fabric to the shore and rinsed it in the ocean. If the piece of fabric chosen for the appliqué was not large enough to cut without a seam, pieces would be joined lengthwise. The appliqué fabric was folded into eighths, and then the border and the center designs were cut. While some quilters preferred a quarter fold, others used the more traditional eighths, and yet in a few cases the central design consisted of four or more separate pieces placed symmetrically around the quilt's center. Because individuality was highly valued, the designer was not limited to such options and many variations arose. [21]

19 Joyce D. Hammond, *Tifaifai and Quilts of Polynesia*. (Honolulu: University of Hawai'i Press, 1986), 14.
20 Christine Faye and Margaret Lovett. *Kaua'i Museum Quilt Collection*. Lihue, Kaua'i, 1991.
21 Wild, 1989.

Similar to methods used in American quilting bees, several women would baste the cut design to the top sheet, starting at the center and working outward to the edges. Generally, however, only the owner of the quilt did the actual appliqué work. Although the stitching used for the appliqué work was usually an overcast stitch, other types of stitching were also used. Also, like the Mainland quilts, batting was inserted between the top sheet and the fabric backing. However a wide variety of fill materials were used in Hawai'i, including soft fibers from *pulu* (tree fern), wool, cotton, and domestic animal hair. As the three layers were stitched together, the quilters started in the quilt's center and worked toward the edges. Quilting frames were set close to the ground so that the quilters could sit on their hand-woven *lau hala* mats. [22]

The first quilting styles-parallel, circular, or diagonal lines - were those taught by the missionaries. Eventually the Hawaiians incorporated stitching styles inspired by their own traditional crafts, such as the woven pattern of their mats, *kapa* designs, and motifs taken from nature, including shells, fish scales, and turtle shells. Some of these quilting styles are believed to be uniquely Hawaiian. From this point, the quilting form evolved into what is now regarded as the traditional Hawaiian technique: stitching that parallels the inner and outer edges of the appliquéd design. This type of contour quilting, also known as echo quilting - called *kuiki lau* in Hawaiian - gives a three-dimensional quality to a quilt, a quality often described as resembling the waves in the ocean. Such wavelike rows of quilting (ideally measuring half an inch apart) give life to the piece and create a complementary motif. [23]

ASYMMETRICAL CONTEMPORARY QUILT
Aloha for Wayne / Patricia Lei Murray
Design, hand appliqué and hand quilting by
Patricia Lei Murray. 28"x41"

22 Wild, 1989.
23 Wild, 1989.

Traditional Hawaiian Quilt Designs

The Hawaiian quilt pattern is usually an allegorical theme, subtly expressed. Often, there is not a clear connection between the actual design and the theme. At other times, the design is a reproduction of an object that strikes the fancy of the designer. Hawaiian women drew heavily on the garden and nature for their quilt patterns. Floral designs are often abstract representations of flowers found on trees, shrubs and plants. Early appliqué designs tended to be fairly simple with much of the background fabric remaining visible, but the designs became progressively bolder and more complex by the end of the nineteenth century. Early designs echoed patterns found on *kapa*, but they gradually moved toward capturing the beauty of plant life and Hawaiian history. Designs inspired by nature were probably the first and most frequently used. Quilters on each of the Islands selected their own island's flowers to be incorporated into their quilts. When new plants were introduced into Hawai'i, their flowers were represented in quilt designs.

The Hawaiian Quilt Research Project has been collecting information, photos and stories associated with quilts produced before 1960. One of the researchers noted:

> We have noticed that there is a crossover in the early Hawaiian quilt patterns. They were not always echo-quilted. We have found grid work, diamond shape grid work. We have what they called "turtleback" quilting technique, which to me is what we called "orange peel" in American patchwork. But here in Hawaiian quilting they are called turtleback. There is the "coin pattern" where there is the coin and the square, which was like a grid, a squared grid with a circle in the middle. ...I would say in the last twenty years or so, you don't see the true echo quilting in both the surface pattern and the background. To save time they'd outline the leaves of the appliqué, and then just do the echo quilting around the pattern like the ripples in a pond, in the background. ...In many of the old time quilts, you would see it all have echo quilting (Sue Chang).

Although Hawaiians learned to quilt from the Americans, there are significant differences between the methods of construction and the resultant Hawaiian quilt styles. Most importantly, American quilts were often constructed by groups of women who worked together in quilting bees. In Hawai'i, however, quilting has traditionally been a solitary practice for Hawaiian women who intentionally worked in isolation. This traditional practice restricted innovation.

TRADITIONAL QUILT
Leinani o Paneki / Sharon Balai
*Design, hand appliqué and hand quilting
by Sharon Balai. 91"x94"*

DESIGNS AND PATTERNS

Over the years, the original designs, the intents of the quilters, and the original names have been lost. In such cases, a recurring theme found in the names of these quilts often gives a clue to the origin. For example, the design generically known as *Ka u'i o Maui* (The Beauty of Maui) has also been named *Lei Roselani* (Heavenly Rose Lei, the rose being the flower of the Island Maui), *Noho o Pi'ilani* (Pi'ilani Ancestry, the Pi'ilani family being a royal family of Maui), *Piko o Haleakalā* (Summit of Haleakalā, Haleakalā being a volcano on Maui), and *Kahului Breakwater* (Kahului is located on the Island of Maui). From these examples it is inferred that the design originated on the Island of Maui. However, a few quilt makers had no reason to refer to Maui when naming their quilts of this design. As a result, the design has also been called Helene's Lei, The Pearl of 'Ewa (on O'ahu), and the Edge of the Rainbow. In most cases, the oldest designs have the most variations and a great variety of names. The inspiration for a particular design was not always reflected in the name given by the quilter. The meanings of Hawaiian quilt patterns were often very subtle, and generally about relationships. Some quilts have a meaning expressed with Hawaiian subtlety, some are allegorical, and others embody a completely private meaning (*kaona*). Sometimes, the meanings were so personal to the quilter that they remain a secret known only to the creator.[24] A good example was provided by Elizabeth Akana who described a pattern known as "Press Gently" that was sometimes made for a wedding gift. The pattern was very abstract until you knew that it was about the sexual act. This quilt, when kept on the marital bed, was intended to remind the new husband to be gentle when making love to his new wife.

In old Hawai'i, a designer's originality was highly valued and a code of ethics arose to protect designs; they were considered to be the exclusive property of the owner, and copying was not to be done without permission. Many quilts were hung on clotheslines with the appliqué side in, so as to prevent the possibility of someone copying the design.[25] Although many quilt makers guarded their designs jealously, still others freely shared their patterns as a mark of friendship. A woman who shared would often do so with the understanding that every quilt made from her pattern would carry the name she had given to it.[26] Others shared their patterns with the understanding that the name of the quilt *per se* would be changed.[27]

24 Jones, 1973.
25 Carlyne Jaffe Stewart. Snowflakes in the Sun: A How-to Guide to Hawaiian Quiltmaking. 1986. Wallace-Homestead Book. Co., Lombard, IL,1986.
26 Dorothy B. Barrere, "Hawaiian Quilting: A Way of Life," The Conch Shell (Honolulu: Bishop Museum Association, 3, No. 2, 1965), 17.
27 Akana, 1981, 43.

Today, some quilters share a design with the entreaty that the new owner should change it to please herself and give it a new name.[28] Historically, jealously-guarded designs were rarely copied without permission of the owner for fear of embarrassment or shame should the "theft" be discovered.[29] As a result of these traditions, many variations and names for a basic design are found. Patterns are the life-blood of traditional Hawaiian quilters. As Margo Morgan stated:

> My very first Hawaiian quilt patterns came from these people in Kahana. ...And I did go to the Wai'anae Library - when it first got its quilt pattern section opened. And I copied patterns there. ...And somehow since then, patterns have just been drifting in my direction. And I now have quite a collection.

It is generally believed that traditional Hawaiian quilts have usually been done in only two colors, but there were occasional examples of old quilts done with more color. Doris Nosaka remembered, "When the old people used to do quilts, they sometimes did three colors. And they did more colors than we can think of, you know." Margo Morgan was given a multi-colored quilt in 1925:

> My very first acquaintance with a Hawaiian quilt was one that was made for me by a person by the name of Alice Mahelona, a lovely Hawaiian lady [in 1925]. And...it was slightly unusual, because it is done in multi-colors. It was a Bird of Paradise, and basically green on white. But the actual flowers were done with the yellow and the blue with the little pink lip. So that it was...rather...unusual to use that many colors in a traditional Hawaiian quilt.

28 Meali'i Kalama quoted in Richard J. Tibbetts, Jr. and Elaine Zinn, *The Hawaiian Quilt A Cherished Tradition*, a 16 mm film. Hawai'i Craftsmen, Honolulu: 1986.

29 Roger G. Rose, *Hawai'i: The Royal Isles*. (Honolulu: Bishop Museum Press, 1980), 176.

TRADITIONAL QUILT
BOMBAX / *Margo Morgan*
Commercial pattern by Kaiki.
Hand appliqué and hand quilting
by Margo Morgan. 87"x87"

MATERIALS AND METHODS

Traditional Hawaiian appliqué quilts have generally been created with two solid colored fabrics, with the appliquéd design done in bright color attached to a pale background. Green, yellow, or red against a white background were the most common combinations for traditional quilts. Occasionally, small patterned fabrics, like calico, appeared in traditional Hawaiian quilts. All work was done by hand, and until recently, quilt battings were made either of wool or cotton.

Hawai'i has never had a textile industry, and because it is 2,500 miles from any other land mass, Hawai'i has been extremely dependant on imported goods. Several times imports ceased altogether in the twentieth century. Historically, the result of this geographic isolation has been a limited availability of fabric and sewing notions and, with other factors, led to a rather homogeneous Hawaiian quilting style.

Traditionally, a Hawaiian quilt design is generally cut on the eighth, meaning that the square pattern paper is folded in half, then half again and again until there are eight sections. The pattern design is cut out, then laid on the single piece of appliqué fabric. When opened up, the design resembles a snowflake and the quilt is basically square. The designs are symmetrical and evenly balanced, so they fill the quilt. Traditional Hawaiian quilts were generally made entirely by hand. Echo quilting was done in white thread, in rows around the appliqué design, like ripples or waves in the water.

TRADITIONAL QUILT
KO KAUA MALA ALOALO I LAHAINA
(LAHAINA GARDENS) / Irene Kubo
Design, hand appliqué and hand quilting
by Irene Kubo. 108"x104"

LEARNING TO QUILT

Although the missionaries began teaching quilting in sewing classes in 1830, soon thereafter quilting instruction left the school and became the responsibility of women in the 'ohana. *Tutu* (grandmothers), mothers and aunties passed down patterns, instructions and rules to the young quilters in the form of *kapu* (taboos). This method of instruction, coupled with a very limited availability of imported fabric and sewing notions, was largely responsible for the stability in the methods, materials and designs found in traditional Hawaiian quilting.

Because Hawaiian quilters worked in isolation they had limited exposure to other ideas and methods. Traditional Hawaiian quilters worked alone at home, and still do today. They generally do not join guilds (as we'll see is common for contemporary Hawaiian quilters), but instead have family networks of female relatives. Although the traditional Hawaiian quilters generally worked alone, their husbands were sometimes involved. "But they didn't do the quilting. They might have helped with the basting, or even with the designs. Later on men helped with taking photographs." (Sue Chang) As Mary Cesar explained, "We learned to do traditional Hawaiian quilting at home, with our families or from a Hawaiian teacher, a *kumu* (a master quilter) and she often has a group of students who basically become part of her 'ohana. *Kumu* quilters have a following and you then have little cliques and they do the same kinds of things, so the traditional Hawaiian quilters have their own networks."

TRADITIONAL QUILT
Koa / Kathy Tripp
Design, hand appliqué and hand quilting by Kathy Tripp. 90"x90"

KAPU AND SPIRITUALITY

Just prior to the arrival of the American missionaries, the Hawaiians' original religious system was eliminated. Called the *kapu* system, it was based on a complex series of rules and taboos (*kapu*) intended to ensure proper respect for the gods, and to protect status differences within Hawaiian society. The *kapu* that men and women could not eat together was intentionally violated in 1819 by Queen Kaʻahumanu and the *kapu* system then was formally eliminated. Nonetheless, *kapu* continued to be important in the cultural system and simply moved from being religious rules enforced by the King, to social norms enforced through the culture as a whole. Mary Cesar stated: "Liholiho and Kaʻahumanu ate together and that officially ended the *kapu*. But *kapu* didn't disappear overnight; they've ruled the way people think. And *kapu* varied from one island to the next. Some quilters will only do some animals but several of us were taught not to do any animals."

Kapu were one of the major forms of instructional methods. *Kapu* could have a spiritual rationale, or a practical nature, based on logic at the time they were instituted. Over time, these became normative processes that may now have no contemporary rationale. Practical *kapu* include the prohibition on quilting at night. Before electric lights, it was logical not to quilt at night. The *kapu* against quilting on black also makes sense because it is simply hard to see the handwork. Other colors can be *kapu* in combination: "I wouldn't put red, yellow and black together on a quilt because those were the *aliʻi* colors (red and yellow were colors of royalty) mixed with a *kapu* color," said one quilter. Quilts weren't to be shown in public before they were finished, and were never to be sat upon. "If I needed help for my quilt, laying it out on the floor, and you know, I can't get on the floor, I would have somebody do it for me. I wouldn't mind them sitting on my quilt because it's just the beginning of the quilt. After you finished the quilt, it's not proper to sit on it. Then it's *kapu*." (Luika Kamaka)

Spiritual *kapu* include the rule that living things such as animals and humans should not be depicted on a quilt. "Animals were seen as too restless, they want to roam so to pin them down is *kapu* because that would capture their spirit." (Kathy Tripp); similarly, "Hawaiians believed the human figures could get up and walk at night" (Mary Cesar). In an interview, Sharon Balai discussed an incident regarding their showing of her husband Kimo's quilt with King Kamehameha's guards depicted in the design: "We put Kimo's quilt on the frame when we did the Sheraton show, and one lady was scolding him 'You're not supposed to do this'.

TRADITIONAL QUILT
*Aloha o Kawaiulani
(My Love for Beth) / Pearl Simmons
Commercial pattern by Kawaiola. Hand
appliqué and hand quilting by Pearl
Simmons. 110"x102"*

...Ours have figures, but it's not for a bed, it's a wall hanging. She was offended because it had the spearman and the *kāhili* bearer on it. There are so many restrictions on what you can and what you cannot do."

One of the most important *kapu* was against sharing patterns. There were numerous reports of women hanging quilts inside out on clotheslines to prevent the quilt pattern from being seen. Sharon Balai reported that, "One of my cousins...burned the patterns when my grandmother died. ...They said that's her patterns and when she die, the patterns supposed to go with her."

While kapu are often quite specific and may deal with spiritual issues, the issue of spirituality can also be much more generalized. For many traditional Hawaiian quilters, there is an intensely spiritual side of quilting.

I have an emotional connection to my quilts and I have to go through a detachment period before giving one away, or selling a quilt. Well, it's hard to explain the spiritual. Meali'i (Kalama) explained being able to design as a gift from God and that He directs your ability to design. In a way it's like listening to your inner self. Sometimes I just can't do anything, and then other times I can sit down and design thirteen new patterns in the same day. It's something we grow up with in Hawaiian culture, the ability to see the spiritual in everything and interpret what we see in our designs. We live with spirituality on a daily basis and you can't separate it from creativity. Like *ho'oponopono* [a method of reaching consensus]. We use spirituality to solve problems. Sometimes I see people do my patterns and it'll look totally different because even though they followed the instructions they didn't know the flower so they couldn't capture it. Sometimes I can tell if the feeling, the spirituality is in the piece. Even local *haoles* (Caucasians) can be in tune with the Hawaiian ways (Mary Cesar).

TRADITIONAL QUILT
HUI HUI PUA / Margo Morgan
Traditional pattern, designer unknown.
Hand appliqué and hand quilting by
Margo Morgan. 105"x105"

TRADITIONAL HAWAIIAN QUILTS: A DEFINITIVE PATTERN

To summarize the previous section, traditional Hawaiian quilts have very distinctive characteristics. The quilts are done mostly by hand rather than machine. They are generally appliquéd in one piece, and done with two contrasting colors. The appliqué design is usually created by folding the one piece of appliqué fabric into eighths before cutting along the folds. By cutting on the eighth, the designs become square and symmetrical. It is often inspired by Hawaiian flowers, environment or a meaningful life-event. Echo quilting is done by hand with white thread in rows that radiate out from the appliqué design. The presence of these characteristics classify a Hawaiian quilt in the traditional category. By comparison, contemporary Hawaiian quilts nearly defy classification.

TRADITIONAL QUILT
Kawaiula Iliahi o Waimea / Margo Morgan
Traditional pattern, designer unknown. Hand
and reverse appliqué and hand quilting by
Margo Morgan. 105"x109"

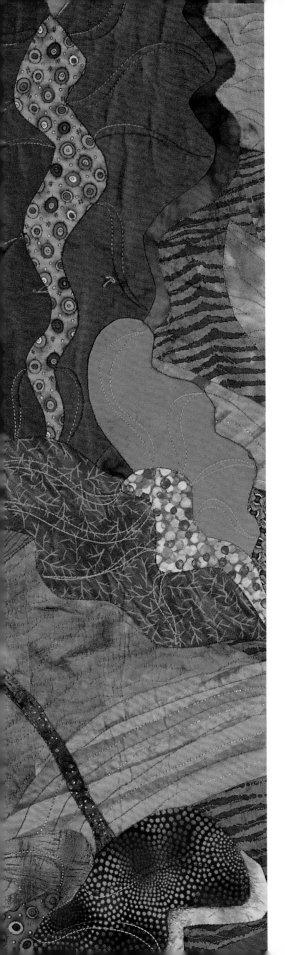

Contemporary Hawaiian Quilts

As a result of a variety of societal changes, quilting went into hibernation between 1945 and the early 1960s, but was kept alive in America's rural areas. Luella Doss notes that it never completely died out. An awareness of the need for individual creativity grew in the 1960s, and quilting moved into the American consciousness as a result of several museum exhibitions that proved to be landmarks in changing American perceptions about quilts. In 1965, the Op Art movement inspired an exhibition on "Optical Quilts" in Newark, New Jersey, leading quilts to be seen for the first time as works of art. [30]

PICTORIAL CONTEMPORARY QUILT

Lazy Maui Lanai / Susan Wachter

Quilt design and machine appliqué by Susan Wachter, machine quilting by Dianna Grundhauser. 46"x61"

30 Luella Doss, Contemporary Quilts. In Dennis Duke and Deborah Harding, *America's Glorious Quilts*. China. Hugh Lauter Levin. 1987. 214-256.

QUASI-TRADITIONAL CONTEMPORARY QUILT
PAPAYA / Dianna Grundhauser
Design, appliqué and machine quilting by
Dianna Grundhauser. 76"x66"

QUASI-TRADITIONAL CONTEMPORARY QUILT
OLAPA / Loretta Pasco
Design, hand appliqué and hand quilting
by Loretta Pasco. 60"x44"

QUASI-TRADITIONAL CONTEMPORARY QUILT
LEI NAHELE / Patricia Lei Murray
Design by Nancy Lee Chong of Pacific
Rim Quilts. Hand appliqué and hand
quilting by Patricia Lei Murray. 28"x41"

31 Laurie Woodard, *Quilts from the Margo Morgan*
   Collection, Mission Houses Museum, Honolulu,
   HI 2001
32 Doss, Contemporary Quilts, 1987. 215.

In 1971, an exhibit at the Whitney Museum of American Art in New York City forever changed the art world's view of quilting. "Abstract Design in American Quilts," presented quilts as art rather than craft, describing them in terms of line and design. This seminal exhibit marked the beginning of the second great quilt revival of the twentieth century.[31] Soon thereafter quilt exhibitions became very popular and quilts began to represent a re-connection with our past. "In the presence of quilts one is made aware of the silent rhythms of life and the songs of the past. The air of warmth and humanity radiated by a display of quilts awoke a need in our culture."[32] Quilts became a symbol of retreat from the technological present into the comfortable, warm and human spirit of the past.

While the transition from traditional quilt forms into art quilts has been steady and relatively deliberate throughout most of America, that has not been the case in Hawai'i. Until World War II, there was one definitive form of Hawaiian quilt, that which has been referred to here as the traditional Hawaiian quilt. When quilting became less common throughout America it continued to be done in Hawai'i, but with significantly fewer quilters. However with the quilting renaissance that began in the late 1970s, it became clear that while traditional

33 Wild, 1989.

Hawaiian quilts were still being made, a new form of Hawaiian quilting was emerging. My task here is to explain how the definitive form of Hawaiian quilting that had been in place for more than a century was able to undergo such a radical change. It seemed that all of a sudden the rules disappeared and anything was possible. The contemporary quilts are stunning, if radically different.

Contemporary Hawaiian quilts are very difficult to categorize. They generally have a tropical or Hawaiian theme, bold colors and appliqué. Beyond that, there are no rules. According to Nina Medeiros, "A lot of my contemporary quilts have three, even four colors. And the fabrics - I've been using polyester cotton and even...chintz. It doesn't have to be just plain hundred percent cotton."

Contemporary Hawaiian quilts can be seen on a continuum from traditional Hawaiian appliqué style through a wide range of contemporary art quilt forms. These categories include quasi-traditional, asymmetrical, pictorial, appliquéd and pieced, and patchwork. The contemporary Hawaiian quilt is focused on making a dramatic visual statement about Hawai'i. The quilts are often realistic and pictorial, more like an artistic canvas in which the viewer can understand what the designer intended. The primary focus of contemporary Hawaiian quilts is as art, whereas with traditional Hawaiian quilts, functionality was dominant and aesthetic expression was secondary.

With such a long-standing traditional art form thoroughly embedded within traditional Hawaiian culture, the question at hand is how did this shift occur? Several causes can be attributed. Changes in the post-World War II period are largely responsible, as this was a time of rapid societal transition in Hawai'i.

In the 1960s and 1970s there was little or no quilting going on here as local women went into the labor force. New materials came in, and so did a big group of *haoles* following statehood. A void was left in the training of quilters. No one was teaching the girls during this time (Mary Cesar).

Similarly, Cleo Kobayashi remembered that "It seemed like no one made quilts here in the 1960s because TV changed the way leisure time was spent. Everyone had TV by then and in the evenings most of the families sat around and watched TV."

43

PARADISE IN BLOOM / *Verginia Marra*
Commercial quilt patterns: Breadfruit, Pineapple, Rose, Maile Lei, Monstera and Crown Flower, by Carol Kamaile; Kukui Nut and Angel Trumpet, by Elizabeth Root; Night Blooming Cereus, by Mary's Treasures. Hand appliqué by Verginia Marra. Machine quilting by Dianna Grundhauser. 75"x75"

OHIA LEHUA / *Lisa Louise Adams*
Design, appliqué and hand quilting by Lisa Louise Adams. 37"x23"

ASYMMETRICAL CONTEMPORARY QUILT
DRAGON QUILT / *Charlene Hughes*
*Design, piecing, hand and machine quilting by
Charlene Hughes. 60"x50"*

Today, Hawaiian quilt making is again practiced with creativity and enthusiasm. New designs are created to memorialize current events, record newly introduced plants, and preserve special memories. Old designs are still used, incorporating subtle alterations that enhance the beauty of each piece, and patterns are shared with warmth and friendship. There are many quilting classes and clubs, there is a thriving commercial pattern industry, and Hawaiian quilts are prominently displayed in museums throughout the state of Hawai'i.[33] While traditional Hawaiian quilters continue to quilt as did their foremothers, contemporary Hawaiian quilters learn the traditional techniques, but express creativity with few constraints.

QUASI-TRADITIONAL CONTEMPORARY QUILT
Nash's Mokihana Lei / Lisa Louise Adams
Traditional pattern designed by Hannah Baker.
Appliqué and hand quilting by Lisa Louise
Adams. 41"x41"

QUASI-TRADITIONAL HAWAIIAN QUILT
Orchids with my Friends / Keri Duke
Designed by Keri Duke and Dianna
Grundhauser. Appliqué by Keri Duke; flower
detail by Iris Yamato, Elle Boughton, Elyn
Worral, Penny Sieling, Penny Dant and Joan
Davis. Machine quilting by Dianna
Grundhauser. 90"x90"

QUASI-TRADITIONAL CONTEMPORARY QUILT
Woodrose / Mary Haunani Cesar
Design, appliqué and hand quilting by Mary Cesar.
Hand dyed fabric by Marit Kucera. 44"x44"

TRAINING CONTEMPORARY QUILTERS

"In the old days we learned to quilt from moms, aunties, *tutu*. The traditional quilters still teach their girls the same way they learned and when they come to my exhibitions they say 'I still have to finish my first quilt that Mom started me on. She's gone now'. So they think about doing another but when I offer to help them with the first one they don't want to take classes. So I say 'try finish that one- your mother would want you to finish it'. Elderly ladies still will only do the traditional style and don't want to come to classes to learn." (Luika Kamaka)

There are fewer young women who want to learn how to create Hawaiian quilts. Sharon remembered: "When I was a child, we used to go to Grandma's and she tried to teach me quilting. I said, I don't want to learn that. I rather go swim in the river. ...I didn't want to learn cause you have to sit in the house all day."

The Territory of Hawai'i became an American state in 1959 and this led to a huge shift in the population, when an influx of people from the U.S. Mainland moved to Hawai'i. Referred to as *haoles*, this group of Euro-Americans were part of a widespread societal shift in Hawai'i. The newcomers enthusiastically embraced Hawaiian arts and crafts. "When we Mainland *haoles* came here after Statehood, we

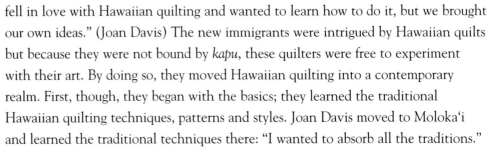

fell in love with Hawaiian quilting and wanted to learn how to do it, but we brought our own ideas." (Joan Davis) The new immigrants were intrigued by Hawaiian quilts but because they were not bound by *kapu*, these quilters were free to experiment with their art. By doing so, they moved Hawaiian quilting into a contemporary realm. First, though, they began with the basics; they learned the traditional Hawaiian quilting techniques, patterns and styles. Joan Davis moved to Moloka'i and learned the traditional techniques there: "I wanted to absorb all the traditions."

Instruction moved from the home into commercial quilting classes. *Kumu* quilters began classes as early as the mid-1950s. One of the first was Meali'i Kalama who was perhaps Hawai'i's best known quilter. Meali'i Kalama was named a National Heritage Fellow by the National Endowment for the Arts Folks Arts Program in 1985. Among her students are Elizabeth Akana and Doris Nosaka. Doris remembered that "when I got married, nobody else was teaching quilting until Meali'i when she started her class in 1955 or 1956." After statehood, "lots of *haoles* and Japanese began quilting and did it through classes and guilds. They learned traditional quilting, but changed it with their own ideas." (Luika Kamaka) "After the tradition nearly died out we started to use hand dyed fabrics with the old patterns and that is where the contemporary Hawaiian quilting began," said a quilter in Volcano. "By using hand-dyed fabrics this gives it a whole new dimension."

I was trained on Molokai over 20 years ago by Johanna Wong Leong. Right afterwards I met and became friends with Auntie Earline McGuire who was a fabulous mentor. Each teacher will pass on different stories and legends. Johanna taught me the '*ulu* (breadfruit) pattern first. '*Ulu* was the staple of the traditional Hawaiian diet. The legend is that if you do the '*ulu* first, you will be assured of a plentiful life and you will continue to do more Hawaiian quilting. There were about ten of us in our Hawaiian quilting class and our homework was to do our appliqué. After quilting our first square we each decided to take a flower design to do next. These squares were then sewn together in what is called a "poho poho" style. We all did the quilting on this first quilt on a large floor

frame at Johanna's house. When we finished the quilt we raffled it and donated quilt books to the Molokai Public Library. The funny thing is that my mother was visiting from the mainland and she is the one who had the winning raffle ticket. So, as it turns out, I still have that quilt and it is filled with memories of our first introduction to Hawaiian quilting.

Traditional quilt teachers insist on students learning to do the breadfruit ('*ulu*) design for their first quilt. Luika first learned to quilt forty years ago but refused to do the '*ulu* pattern. "The first quilt that I wanted to do was a pink hibiscus." To avoid a conflict with the teacher, she helped other people in the class instead of working on an '*ulu* pattern. "Then about the week before the class was over, I designed my own hibiscus. I had bought pink and black but was told that I couldn't use black…. So I went out and bought something that was on sale, which was the gold color. So pink and gold was my first quilt, and that was a hibiscus, not an '*ulu*. Even so, I've produced a lot of quilts and only recently did an '*ulu*."

In the early 1980s, Hawaiian quilters began to incorporate more color. "There was a young group of quilters (in their 30s and 40s) they were still pretty traditional but in the classes, they were beginning to branch out with more colors or make different flowers in different colors. They weren't pushing the bounds much but they were beginning to do some new things." (Mary Cesar) Following that, quilt teachers began encouraging experimentation. Kathy Tripp said "Here's what I teach: I say this is the way it's originally taught. But in contemporary Hawaiian quilting, we explore. We want the young people to be innovative."

QUASI-TRADITIONAL CONTEMPORARY QUILT
Rain Forest / *Sue Chang*
Commercial pattern Laua'e by Kawaiola. Hand appliqué and hand quilting by Sue Chang. 41"x53"

Although most contemporary female Hawaiian quilters learn through classes, another element of their education comes from the quilt guild, which plays a significant role in the lives of these women. Not only do quilters learn new and different techniques, the guilds provide for a great deal of inspiration. In American quilting, guilds have provided women with support groups and significant social networks. Until contemporary Hawaiian quilters brought in the concept of guilds, Hawaiian quilters worked in isolation; this may have contributed to the lack of innovation in the traditional Hawaiian quilt forms. Contemporary Hawaiian quilting is a social activity with a group, and the quilters share their work as it's happening. Consequently, quilts can change and evolve as they are created. "Being involved in guilds, being more aware gives you more possibilities. It brings in more Mainland influences," said Dianna Grundhauser who continued:

> Quilting in isolation, the way traditional Hawaiian quilters do keeps the tradition going and stifles change. These quilters have a desire to keep that tradition alive. Some just really don't like patchwork or other methods. They don't take classes or belong to guilds. Most of the traditional quilters have relatives who quilt and have handed down the skills through the family. Their attraction to the quilt and family goes together. They learn to quilt from family. It's about their heritage, and it's important to the Hawaiians to keep that alive.

QUASI-TRADITIONAL CONTEMPORARY QUILT
Mele Kakikimaka / Charlene Hughes
Design, appliqué and hand quilting by Charlene Hughes. Copyright 1997, Charlene Hughes.108"x90"

QUASI-TRADITIONAL CONTEMPORARY QUILT
Hana Pa'a / Kimo Balai
Designed by Sharon Balai. Hand appliqué and
hand quilting by Kimo Balai. 84"x104"

IGNORING THE KAPUS; STRETCHING THE BOUNDS

Describing the core of contemporary Hawaiian quilting, Jane remarked that "In the last ten to fifteen years we have new themes coming up that ignore the *kapus*. Often, it's men who are doing this. Male quilters are more interested in using animals in their motifs, where traditionally we weren't allowed to have them".

In traditional Hawaiian quilting, men had a history of helping their wives quilt, but in the contemporary realm male quilters drive the process and design and create quilts on their own. Unlike most of the contemporary female Hawaiian quilters who learned to quilt by taking classes and participating in guild activities, men more often learned to quilt in a less formal way. Unless they were raised by an Hawaiian quilter, male quilters are more likely to have been self-taught and used books and magazines to get started. Following that informal introduction, men are likely to take an occasional class in order to learn specific techniques. Luika Kamaka

QUASI-TRADITIONAL CONTEMPORARY QUILT
Kilauea Iki / Lincoln Okita
Design adapted from traditional pattern by
Hannah Baker. Appliqué and hand quilting by
Lincoln Okita. 96"x96"

QUASI-TRADITIONAL CONTEMPORARY QUILT

*He Mala Pua Loke o ka Wahine Mo'i /
Ric Stark*

*Designed by Ric Stark and Allan James.
Appliqué and hand quilting by Ric Stark.
107"x107"*

is Hawaiian and had four sons. "I taught my four sons to quilt and design; we'd sit down in the evening and work on a quilt - each boy on a corner. They're into dolphins and turtles. Guys now do a lot of animal designs but that used to be *kapu*."

Male quilters working in the contemporary Hawaiian genre typically learned to quilt by themselves. Lincoln Okita is one such quilter. He acknowledged that "one of the benefits of being self taught is not being hampered by old rules." For awhile, he and his wife lived near an Indian reservation where "we fell in love with the star quilts made by the Sioux. I loved the designs but not the quality of the work." So Lincoln decided to learn to quilt. "Even though I'm from Hawai'i

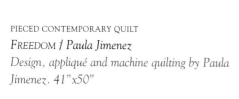

PIECED CONTEMPORARY QUILT

Freedom / Paula Jimenez

*Design, appliqué and machine quilting by Paula
Jimenez. 41"x50"*

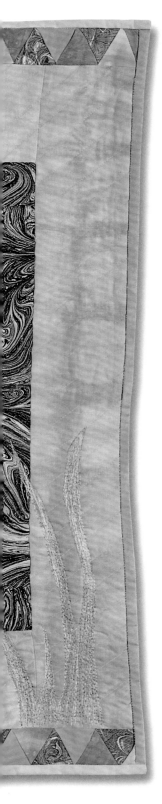

there are no quilters in my family, so we were on our own. We had to travel 90 miles to Pierre to buy fabric and bought a book through mail order. ...Once Jo and I figured out how to do patchwork and I built the frame I began patchwork quilting. Then when we moved back home I got into Hawaiian appliqué."

Stan Yates is a scientist who lives on Kaua'i. He is an innovative quilter who learned by watching his wife do traditional Hawaiian quilting. When she finished the first quilt after their marriage,

I was just astounded by the workmanship and the size of it, and the beauty of it. It was in two colors, as I recall. And that got me started on the Hawaiian quilt as an art form. And I began to think about designs in my mind. And my wife would say, Oh that wouldn't work, or that wouldn't look good, or you couldn't do that with fabric. Or something like that. But it intrigued me so much that I got some books, I read about designs, I looked at designs of the quilts that I saw around me at the Kaua'i Museum and elsewhere. And finally took the step to ask my wife to show me how to make a quilt. Really, there's only two steps. You do an appliqué stitch, and you do a quilting stitch. So I started with the quilting stitch, and something that she cut out for me. And had a terrible time and realized it was much harder than I thought it was gonna be, but it was a challenge. And I kept at it, and after I learned how to quilt, then I learned how to appliqué. And then I was able to take the designs that I had created in my mind and to cut them out and put them on another piece of fabric, and to really produce my own quilt.

APPLIQUÉD AND PIECED CONTEMPORARY QUILT
Ae'o Pond / Zee Sarr
Design, appliqué, piecing and hand quilting
by Zee Sarr. 33"x43"

While there are a few men in the Hawaiian quilt guilds, men are more likely to work alone than to be more than superficially involved in guilds. As Dianna Grundhauser stated: "Men are beginning to get into it here on Maui; they're just learning to do Hawaiian quilting. Some are young men; there's Jay Wilson, he's an artist who does tapestries and mosaics. Another man is in his mid-30s and a stay at home dad. Men do more geometrics, more engineered looking things." That pattern is true on the other islands as well. "I try to be as realistic as I can with the flowers, the turtle; I think when you get too abstract you lose a bit," said Lincoln. "It may be a male thing to get more realistic. Quilting allows me to withdraw into myself; I can listen to a ball game and quilt but if I get distracted I'll prick my finger. I wouldn't describe myself as a Hawaiian quilter, but as a local quilter who loves doing Hawaiian quilting." Mary Cesar observed: "Men are more likely to do animal designs and use themes that ignore the *kapu*. Men are willing to venture beyond the traditional techniques, designs and colorations."

I wanted to have a variation in colors, though I know there are some folks who don't think we should go beyond the traditional style. I enjoy having a variety of colors in the piece. I found I could manipulate the fabric to do that. Then I began going into more variety of colors in the piece itself. Once I got going on this I realized there was something different. I got into batik fabrics that I really like. For one piece, I needed a mixture of greens and yellows and found it in a batik, and figured it'd work, but it kinda looked awful. Once I got working on it then it began to develop—each time you start quilting it begins to develop a totally different kind of personality—each step changes the quilt and by the time it is finished it may be totally different (Lincoln Okita).

QUASI-TRADITIONAL CONTEMPORARY QUILT
PIKAKE AND TUBEROSE | Lincoln Okita
Design copied from traditional pattern by Hannah Baker and reduced in size by Elizabeth Akana. Appliqué and hand quilting by Lincoln Okita. 64"x64"

ASYMMETRICAL CONTEMPORARY QUILT
Thistles in the Garden / *Elizabeth Akana*
Design, appliqué and hand quilting by Elizabeth
Akana. 35"x31"

The freedom to experiment seems to be important to the contemporary Hawaiian quilters who are male. Stan remarked:

Lately I've seen more flexibility, if you will, in terms of using more colors or using marine shapes, fish shapes, things like that. And...I would say that it appears to me that just as with almost any other art form or art type, one sees an evolution of design and of sophistication. In my own way it's trying to do more with two colors. ...I know that I'm always aware of trying to stay within the boundaries of the art form, yet to be somewhat flexible within those boundaries. And I'm beginning to see some of that same thing; a double border or colors that would be more characteristic of Amish rather than Hawaiians. It really is a challenge to be able to do something that's interesting with just two colors.

COLOR CHIRAL / *Jane
Loeffler*
*Design created by Jane
in a workshop taught by
Caryl Bryer Fallert.
Machine piecing and
quilting by Jane
Loeffler. 24"x18"*

66

ASYMMETRICAL
CONTEMPORARY QUILT
*ANTHURIUM / Jane
Loeffler*
*Design created by Jane
in a workshop taught by
Caryl Bryer Fallert.
Machine piecing and
quilting by Jane
Loeffler. 24"x33"*

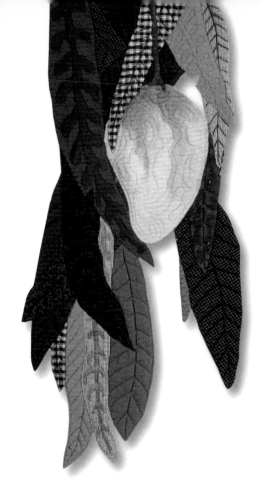

KAPU AND SPIRITUALITY

In order to freely design, most contemporary Hawaiian quilters pay little heed to the traditional *kapu*. Joan Davis did traditional Hawaiian quilting and, according to Dianna, "Now she's broken all the rules, all the *kapu*. Her work is spectacular!" Some quilters see practical kapus as being easier to ignore: Dianna said: "Black for a background is a departure, it used to be *kapu*. But some of those were really about what was available or difficult. In a way it was like advice, it's just so hard to quilt on black." Similarly, Luika said, "I think I broke a lot of rules, a lot of tradition. I know I'm to blame for it. But I kind of feel happy that I did. I'm not superstitious. I like using black which is a beautiful color."

Some of the contemporary Hawaiian quilters encountered resistance in the 1970s, because they were breaking *kapu*, but even today the *kapu* still are culturally loaded. Ric Stark recently finished a very large, complex quilt. His auntie helped him with the quilt. She is a traditional Hawaiian quilter and told him to: "only quilt at home; only get it out when you're working on it; don't show it; don't go to classes; it's just you and me until you finish this."

Kapu are the source of what friction exists between the traditional and contemporary quilters. For example, Mary Cesar noted that "Some of the traditional quilters have had problems with my making the Pele quilt. [Pele is the goddess of the volcano]. I don't see it as a problem because it's not a traditional pattern. Some might be concerned that because I'm part Hawaiian I should not have done this but I did pray to Pele for guidance."

ASYMMETRICAL CONTEMPORARY QUILT
Cloud Forest Shell Ginger /
Luna Edwards
Design, machine appliqué and quilting
by Luna Edwards. 22"x24"

Luika noted: " There's a sensual and spiritual side of Hawaiian quilts. I like to draw big, to put myself in the quilt. I feel the vibes and put it into the pattern. The center of the quilt is myself on the land; the echo quilting is the ripples on the water. I am a child of the land (*keiki o ka 'āina*). My spirit is in it, like *mana*. *Mana* is like a feeling from me to the person I design for. I put my love into the quilt. And when it comes out like what they wanted-it's chicken skin [goose bumps]!" However, other quilters believe there's been a loss of spirituality in contemporary Hawaiian quilting:

Pele was an interesting quilt. I asked Pele for permission to make the quilt. I figured if I had a lot of *pilikia* [problems] I would just quit because it wasn't meant to be but instead it was almost too easy. It went together really fast and great and it came out exactly as I had wanted. I figured I had help from Pele or that wouldn't have happened. I had this dream that she wanted her name on the quilt but I wasn't working on it at the time (I hadn't started quilting the borders) and the quilt had been shown without the borders being quilted. So I was getting ready to show it again a year and a half later. I was staying at a friend's house in Kona, but doing a show at Waikōloa and hadn't quilted all the border and needed to get it done. I needed to mark another section first but I couldn't get to my pencils...they were locked in the van. Then I dreamed about Pele wanting her name on the quilt. And the next day I left the stencil at the hotel and couldn't get to it even if I wanted. And I had the dream again. So I quilted Pele's name in the quilt and she's been happy ever since (Mary Cesar).

PICTORIAL CONTEMPORARY QUILT
Pele Honua Mea / Mary Haunani Cesar
Design inspired by the art work of Herb Kane. Machine applique, hand and machine quilting by Mary Cesar. 60"x60"

ASYMMETRICAL

CONTEMPORARY QUILT

PELE / Elizabeth Akana
Design, appliqué and
hand quilting by
Elizabeth Akana.
34"x21"

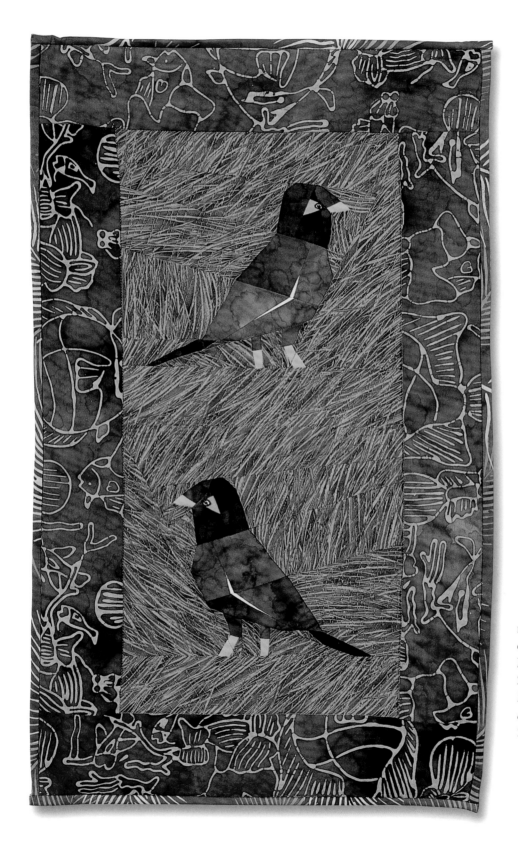

PICTORIAL
CONTEMPORARY QUILT
Mynas in the Grass /
Zee Sarr
Design, machine piecing
and machine quilting by
Zee Sarr. 22"x14"

PICTORIAL CONTEMPORARY QUILT
MEYER SUGAR MILL / Joan Davis
Design by Joan Davis, appliqué by
Joan Davis and Ada De Courcey,
machine quilting by Dianna
Grundhauser. 80"x90"

CONTEMPORARY DESIGNS AND PATTERNS

For some Hawaiian quilters, spirituality and design go hand in hand. Several report that quilt designs come to them in their dreams. Luika noted "when I go to bed, I dream my pattern out. I'm fortunate that I'm gifted with this, you know. Because I can dream up a lot of patterns." Similarly, Hawai'i's well-known quilter Elizabeth Akana stated that "If I have trouble with a pattern, I just put it out of my mind and it will be resolved in my dreams that night. I will wake up with a solution to the problem." She also recalled that Meali'i Kalama believed that spirituality and designing were intimately connected. Although Elizabeth is known as a contemporary quilter, she's been described as equally adept at traditional Hawaiian quilting. "Her designs have a contemporary twist to the traditional, yet there's something to them that separates them from the old time patterns. She's traditional in her elements." (Joan Davis)

MEYER SUGAR MILL

1878

KALA'E - MOLOKA'I

Alan James is a formally trained artist who works in both apparel and textiles. His work was described by Ric Stark as "contemporary *kahiko* (old or ancient style) - he pushes us forward by taking us back to ancient Hawaiian culture." Alan designed the quilt that Ric made for his mother. Ric stated that: "Alan describes this as the hardest thing artistically that he's ever done. He's the artist but it was in my head. It went from my mind into his and out through his hands into the design. An important goal for Alan is to perpetuate Hawaiian culture. "My auntie gave me strict guidelines that I wasn't to do this for money because that's not Hawaiian, but it's really to share the *mana'o* [thought, meanings]." Hawaiian quilts are about aloha, about love. "Making a quilt, you think of the person and then focus on the relationship and it just flows!" said Lincoln Okita.

New quilters whose families were not from Hawai'i did not have ready access to Hawaiian quilt patterns until some were eventually made public. "The fact that the old patterns are hard to get may have something to do with the new designs coming out," said Linda.

When I moved here, patterns were few and far between, especially for larger quilts. Although you could trace the old bed size patterns at the Waianae Library and the Kamuela quilt show, there weren't any new patterns available so I started making my own. The first bed size quilt pattern I did I saw on Elizabeth Akana's TV series on PBS. PBS forwarded my letter to the quilter, Annette Sumada, who generously sent me the pattern "Rains of Manoa" which was in the collection of her guild in Hilo. Despite the ease in which I received this pattern, I think most are very closely guarded (Dianna Grundhauser).

PICTORIAL CONTEMPORARY QUILT
MAUI NO KA OI / Micky Palmer
Design, appliqué and hand quilting by
Micky Palmer. 72"x60"

PICTORIAL CONTEMPORARY QUILT

FABULOUS FAKES AND FINNY FRIENDS / Joan McDonald

Design, appliqué, embellishment and machine quilting by
Joan McDonald. 55"x47"

PICTORIAL CONTEMPORARY QUILT
TURTLES AT MALA WHARF / *Joan Davis*
Design, appliqué, embellishment and machine quilting by
Joan Davis. 58"x68"

ASYMMETRICAL CONTEMPORARY QUILT
One Can Never Have Too Much Aloha /
Patricia Lei Murray
Design, applique, hand and machine quilting by
Patricia Lei Murray. 29"x27"

PICTORIAL CONTEMPORARY QUILT
Petroglyph Quilt / Vanessa Sales
Design, hand applique, machine piecing,
and hand quilting by Vanessa Sales.
43"x35"

Contemporary Hawaiian quilts involve major creative decisions in the design process, often in a slow movement away from tradition. Said Joan Davis, "My first departure was a three color chrysanthemum quilt - a memorial quilt commemorating an airline disaster where we lost fourteen kids from Moloka'i. This was a real departure because of the amount of quilting - all the individual leaves were quilted. After that was my sugar mill quilt, and that's multi-layered adding things as you go, it's not cut on the whole." According to Dianna, "the hardest thing about designing a Hawaiian quilt pattern is connecting all the elements. If you have a good eye you can get the balance."

The most dramatic change in contemporary Hawaiian quilts is that they have a great deal of color compared to traditional Hawaiian quilts. Kathy Tripp owns Kilauea Kreations near Volcanoes National Park on Hawai'i. She noticed that "people coming into the shop want really bright colors. Bright colors are identified with Hawai'i and that's what people want. But then we do get people from Japan and they like quilts with intense color." [34]

[34] Individual quilters and quilt shops will take custom orders. It takes approximately a year to make a large traditional Hawaiian quilt with between 100 and 200 hours to do the appliqué, between 300-800 hours to do the echo quilting. Materials run approximately $400 for the quilt; total cost runs from $5,000 to $10,000 for a bed sized quilt.

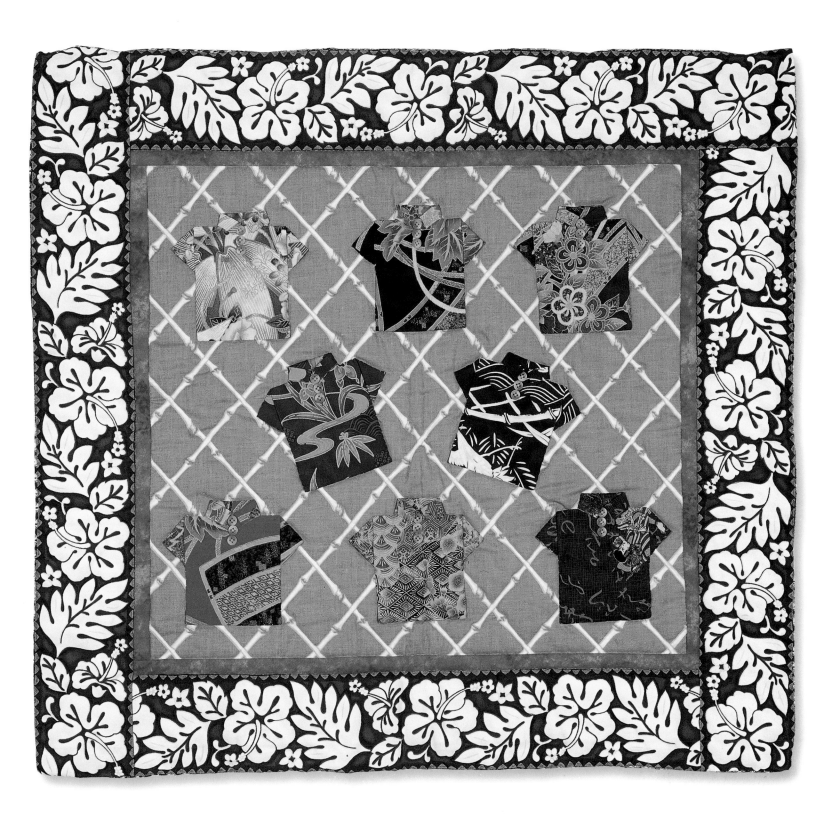

When designing a quilt pattern, there is a contextual frame that the artist works with, in trying to communicate an idea. A contemporary Hawaiian quilter will use whatever techniques or materials are necessary to get that idea across. Mary Cesar did a quilt she called *Mālamalama*, which is about the light coming from traditional *kukui* nut lamps. She needed light radiating from the quilt and found the solution in a hand-dyed fabric so the light was graded, with intense light in the middle. Linda Spencer put it succinctly when she said:

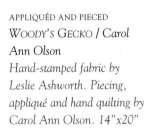

> Creativity and innovation are an outgrowth of a need to solve a particular problem. For instance, I wanted to have three-dimensional bromeliads with flexible leaves. I made leaves of fabric, made them inside out, then inserted wire that could be used to provide shape. We have these juices that are flowing that just MUST be expressed as we solve design problems—sometimes they get us up in the middle of the night and have to be satisfied.

APPLIQUÉD AND PIECED
Woody's Gecko / Carol Ann Olson
Hand-stamped fabric by Leslie Ashworth. Piecing, appliqué and hand quilting by Carol Ann Olson. 14"x20"

UNUSUAL APPLIQUÉ CONTEMPORARY QUILT
Joy of Bromiliads / Linda Spencer
Design and hand quilting by Linda Spencer.
13"x19"

83

PICTORIAL CONTEMPORARY QUILT

TREASURE FROM THE SEA / *Polly Pieropan Boelter*

84   *Design, hand appliqué and hand quilting by Polly Pieropan Boelter. 28"x33"*

PICTORIAL CONTEMPORARY QUILT
Kapinga Morning / Polly Pieropan Boelter
Design, hand appliqué and hand quilting by
Polly Pieropan Boelter. 43" x 30".

85

ASYMMETRICAL CONTEMPORARY QUILT
PUA LANI / Joan McDonald
Design, hand appliqué and hand quilting by
Joan McDonald. 35"x29"

MATERIALS AND METHODS

The revival of quilting has led to a growth of technology related to helping contemporary quilters to design and construct innovative quilts. The textile industry came out with a dacron polyester fiberfill, the first new quilt filler since the eighteenth century. The industry has begun to focus on quilters as a market unto themselves, and now produces a vast array of textiles to suit any quilter's desire. Giant looms can produce very wide fabrics that don't need to be seamed in order to create a wide quilt.

Unique and innovative fabrics are vital to the production of a contemporary Hawaiian quilt. "Sometimes we dye our own fabrics, because that adds a lot. So does the marbled fabric that you can buy, it adds a lot to the quilt," said one of the Volcano quilters. Hand-dyed fabrics are favorites of contemporary quilters, because they can experiment with the varied shadings. Fabrics that are hand dyed to have a central intensity can be used in the center of a design. When a quilter sees another person's experimentation, "Then you're more willing to use what you think will work," said Irene. Lincoln remarked that: "I think using different fabrics and even designing fabrics is really fun—it helps create the meaning you want in your quilt. Experimenting is interesting. I've gone without folding patterns, and just taking the pieces and placing them on the fabric. I like some of the traditional ideas and adding my ideas."

Quilters now have a wide variety of new tools and materials at their disposal. Rotary cutters, self-healing Teflon cutting boards, metal and plastic templates, varied thimbles and needles have been quite useful, in addition to continual refinements in sewing machines and long-arm quilting machines. There are many innovative products that help stimulate ideas and provide help with technical problems. "Every week there's a new tool or fabric or notions to make quilting easier. It's growing because the quilting industry itself is growing. Computers and printers can help us increase or decrease designs," said Jane.

As tools and technology improve, new techniques to facilitate the design process are introduced as well. Paper piecing, fused appliqué and temporary glues (used to

APPLIQUÉD AND PIECED
CONTEMPORARY QUILT
FISHY FRIENDS / *Linda Spencer*
Design, piecing and hand quilting
by Linda Spencer. 57"x65"

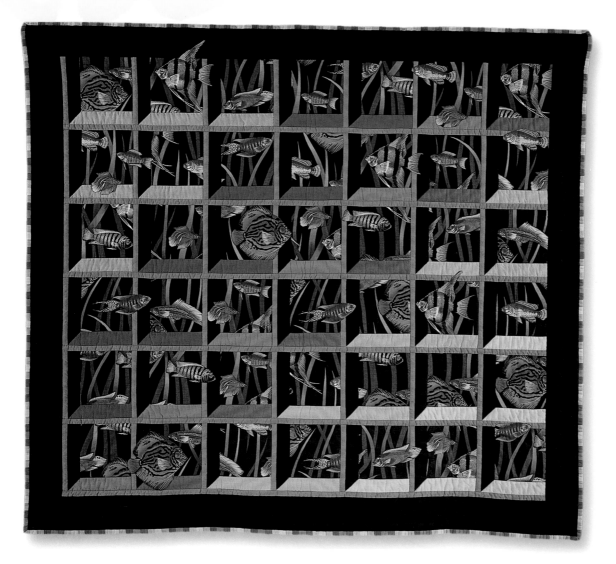

APPLIQUÉD AND PIECED
CONTEMPORARY QUILT
MALIHINI ALOHA / *Mary*
Haunani Cesar
Round Robin quilt.
Individual blocks made by
Faye Labanaris, Ellen
Peters, Jennifer Kaye,
Ellen Crocker, Kathy
Tripp, and Mary Cesar.
Hand and machine quilting
by Mary Cesar. 45"x54"

APPLIQUÉD AND PIECED
CONTEMPORARY QUILT
*THE GIRL AND THE
WATER / Nancy Meyer*
*Design, appliqué and
machine quilting by
Nancy Meyer. 55"x34"*

PICTORIAL CONTEMPORARY QUILT
MANGOS / Joan Davis
Design, hand appliqué and hand quilting on hand-dyed fabrics by Joan Davis. 1999. Photograph by Paul Kodama. Hawai`i State Foundation on Culture and the Arts. 4322-00. 56"x47"

As tools and technology improve, new techniques to facilitate the design process are introduced as well. Paper piecing, fused appliqué and temporary glues (used to minimize basting) are among the innovations that have arisen to help speed up the construction process. Yet again, other techniques have arisen to provide visual interest, such as three-dimensional appliqué and reverse appliqué. "Mary does innovative things with techniques, like stuffed 3-D flowers. She came up with this by taking classes in different techniques and styles. She was trying to do the lehua blossom for the Pele quilt and she used Solvy (a wash away stabilizer) and it worked; experimenting is the way the contemporary quilts evolve." (Kathy Tripp)

APPLIQUÉD AND PIECED CONTEMPORARY QUILT
Hawai'i Quilt Guild Banner
Design, appliqué, piecing and quilting by the Hawai'i Quilt Guild (Honolulu). 60"x80"

APPLIQUÉD AND PIECED CONTEMPORARY QUILT
Volcano Community Quilt
Made in 1988 with hand dyed fabric on the backgrounds, sashing and borders. Quilters and designers from the first row (top left): Bamboo by Bonnie Bissen; Plumeria by Lois Kiehl; Hydrangea by Vanessa Sales. Second row: Ohia by Carol Manoha; Hibiscus by Nora Kawachi; Acacia Koa by Dina Wood Kageler. Third row: Naupaka by Loretta Pasco, adapted from a Konia design; Sashiko lava flow with Kamehameha butterfly and Wawaeiole in chenille by Roberta Baker; Calla Lily by Jelena Clay. Fourth row: Bamboo by Wendy Degenhart; Hydrangea by anonymous Volcano quilter; Uluhe by Kathy Tripp. 57"x75"

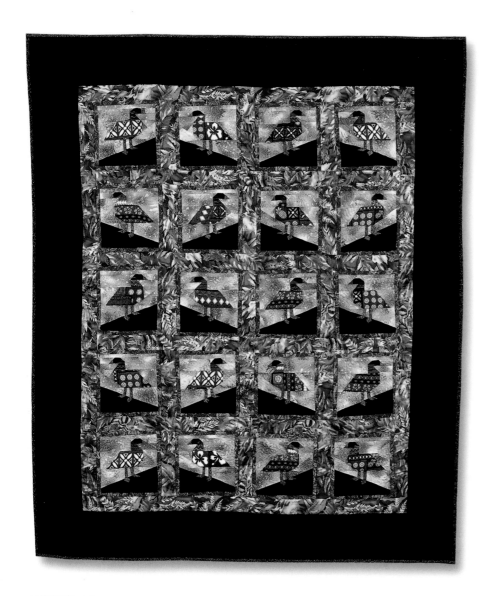

APPLIQUÉD AND PIECED CONTEMPORARY QUILT
Nene Crossing / Zee Sarr
Design, machine piecing, machine quilting by
Zee Sarr. 62"x52"

ASYMMETRICAL CONTEMPORARY QUILT
*Na Keiki o ka Aina (Children of the
Land) / Dina Kageler*
*Hand-printed fabrics, piecing, and hand
quilting by Dina Kageler. 21"x27"*

94

ribbons, beads and other embellishments have changed the art form. Contemporary Hawaiian quilters will machine quilt rather than be bound by handwork.

In addition to quilt guilds, the contemporary quilter has a number of other support networks as well. Workshops, classes, newsletters and a huge gamut of quilting publications provide inspiration and instruction. Materials are easily available for purchase through websites, so that now quilters are not limited by locally available materials. "Staying on top of what's going on in the bigger quilt world is important- taking classes is the best because it gives you a chance to use the new products and ideas. When we go to the Houston show and we see all those quilts and then go shopping after that and buy hand-dyed stuff and they give us all kinds of ideas." (Kathy Tripp)

PIECED CONTEMPORARY QUILT

TUNNEL OF TREES / *Maizie Akimoto*

Design created by Maizie, in a workshop taught by Ruth B. McDowell. Piecing and machine quilting by Maizie Akimoto. 29"x37"

PIECED CONTEMPORARY QUILT

KULA VISTA / *Maizie Akimoto*

Design created by Maizie in a workshop taught by Ruth B. McDowell, using a photo by Elliot V. Smith (Beautiful Hawaii, 1978). Piecing and machine quilting by Maizie Akimoto. 44"x47"

STYLES OF CONTEMPORARY QUILTING

As a result of the variety of influences coming into Hawai'i in the past few decades, contemporary Hawaiian quilts have evolved into a variety of forms. These new quilts have a tropical or Hawaiian theme but generally involve a great deal of color and a wide variety of techniques and creativity. "Contemporary Hawaiian quilters are really into experimenting. Many see themselves first and foremost as artists," said Charlene Hughes. Amazing variations on Hawaiian quilting are being done in other countries, especially Japan. The Japanese are combining American and Hawaiian methods, such as doing patchwork for the whole background but using appliqué on the top.

It is difficult to categorize contemporary Hawaiian quilting because the lack of rules constraining the art form leads to great variety in the quilts that are produced. If we begin with the traditional Hawaiian appliqué quilt, we can see a progression away from the clearly defined hand-made appliquéd quilt toward American art quilts made primarily with sewing machines. The contemporary Hawaiian quilts are seen below on a continuum from the traditional Hawaiian quilt on one end, to the art quilt on the other.

The quasi-traditional Hawaiian quilt is generally a variation of the traditional Hawaiian quilt in that it is of an appliqué design created by a folded pattern technique. The quilt may have a traditional pattern in an unusual color combination, or it may use different fabrics. It may have been designed on the fourth rather than the eighth, leading to a rectangular rather than square design. Generally the quasi-traditional quilt will have many similarities to the traditional, especially in terms of having a large appliqué design and hand quilting surrounding the design.

PIECED CONTEMPORARY QUILT
Of Sand, Beaches, and Dunes /
Nancy Meyer
Design inspired by The Quilters Book of Design *by Ann Johnston. Machine piecing and quilting by Nancy Meyer. 60"x51"*

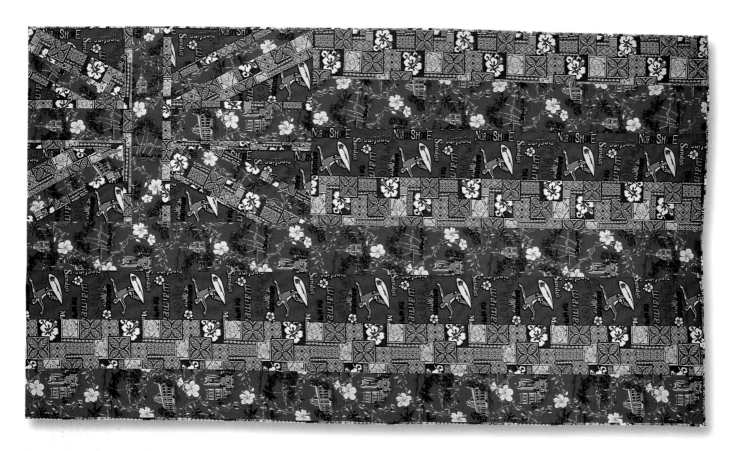

PIECED CONTEMPORARY QUILT
THE STATE OF ALOHA / *Jay Wilson*
Design, piecing and yarn-tying by Jay Wilson.
56"x108"

PIECED CONTEMPORARY QUILT
CONTEMPORARY CONFUSION / *Linda Lewis*
Design, painting, piecing and quilting by Linda Lewis. 17"x18"

PIECED CONTEMPORARY QUILT
MAUI ORCHIDS AT SUNSET / *Shel Jensen*
Design by Caryl Bryer Fallert. Machine piecing and hand quilting by Shel Jensen. 24"x24"

102

Asymmetrical appliqué quilts are often designed so that the left and right sides are different in the design theme, whereas traditional Hawaiian quilts are always symmetrical and formally balanced with each quadrant identical to the others.

Pictorial appliqué quilts are designed much like a picture; the quilt backing is used as an artist's canvas to represent a scene of lsland life. These quilts are generally asymmetrically balanced as well.

Unique appliqué techniques are found on some contemporary Hawaiian quilts. These include three-dimensional appliqués, reverse appliqué (in which the design comes through the foreground from the background fabric), fused (rather than sewn) appliqué and double-sided appliqué quilts.

Appliquéd and pieced quilts represent a transition from the traditional Hawaiian reliance on appliqué as a major design method to the integration of the American pieced or patchwork techniques. In these quilts, the appliqué becomes less and less central to the overall design.

Patchwork quilts are seen in contemporary Hawaiian quilts, representing a near total departure away from Hawaiian traditional techniques. Nina Medeiros predicted this in 1992 when she said: "I think I can take Hawaiian quilting as far as it goes. And eventually it will cross over into the American quilting because of the fabrics and the designs that I will be using." In some cases, contemporary Hawaiian quilting has done just that at least in terms of techniques, yet the themes and coloration are still uniquely Hawaiian.

PIECED CONTEMPORARY QUILT
Red Sails at Night / Shel Jensen
Design from a pattern printed in
Australian Patchwork & Quilting
magazine. Machine piecing by Shel
Jensen, machine quilted by Dianna
Grundhauser. 27"x27"

UNUSUAL APPLIQUÉ CONTEMPORARY QUILT

ULU MAU ALOHA (LOVE UNCONDITIONAL) - SIDE I

Designed, pieced, and particially appliquéd and quilted by Elizabeth A. Akana. Appliqué by Nina Medeiros, and quilted by Kathie Dallas. "That love or Aloha is spoken of in this quilt. Ulu (breadfruit) in Hawaiian means to grow and Mau means always or unceasing. A growing unceasing love/Love Unconditional." (Elizabeth A. Akana) Photo by Sharon Risedorph
62"x62"

UNUSUAL APPLIQUÉ CONTEMPORARY QUILT

ULU MAU ALOHA (LOVE UNCONDITIONAL) - SIDE II

Pieced, appliquéd and partially quilted by Elizabeth A. Akana, who said, "I believe that every quilt has, simply, this side or that, not a front or back. This is the other side of Ulu Mau Aloha/Love Unconditional. It was for a very special friend who will always be loved." Photo by Sharon Risedorph
62"x62"

PIECED CONTEMPORARY QUILT

SYMPTOMS OF AN ARTIST (MAUI MOONS) /
Charlene Hughes

Design by Jay Wilson. Piecing, appliqué and hand quilting by Charlene Hughes. 1998. Photograph by Paul Kodama. Hawai`i State Foundation on Culture and the Arts. 3469-00. 75"x75"

UNUSUAL APPLIQUÉ CONTEMPORARY QUILT
JONATHAN (MY WAY) - SIDE II
Designed, appliquéd and finished by Elizabeth
A. Akana, quilted by Kathie Dallas. This quilt
refers to the book Jonathan Livingston Seagull.
It reminds us all to be all that we can be, that
indeed we do not have to fly with the flock but
can instead be our own bird. 58"x68"

UNUSUAL APPLIQUÉ CONTEMPORARY QUILT
JONATHAN (MY WAY) - SIDE I
Designed, appliquéd and finished by Elizabeth A. Akana,
quilted by Kathie Dallas. The flock of gulls that Jonathan
dared to stray from are subtly seen on side I but are boldly
represented on side II. Photo by Sharon Risedorph
58"x68"

UNUSUAL APPLIQUÉ CONTEMPORARY QUILT
Aloha Oe IV - side I & II
Designed and Quilted by Elizabeth Akana
42"x42"

UNUSUAL APPLIQUÉ CONTEMPORARY QUILT
Lei Roselani / Dianna Grundhauser
Design, appliqué, hand quilting by Dianna
Grundhauser. Dimensional rose designs from
Dimensional Appliqué, by Elly Sienkiewicz.
62"x62"

110

CONCLUSIONS

In spite of the pressures to lean toward American quilting, Hawaiian quilting will, I believe, retain essential elements of the traditional Hawaiian quilts in that they derive from the uniquely beautiful place we call Hawai'i. Luika may have summed it up best when she said, "Designing a Hawaiian quilt is like drawing a picture, or painting a scene of O'ahu. ...I think it's within the individual and shows how they feel. ...There's something exciting in Hawaiian quilting. And so I don't think it's a dying art."

One shift I would predict is that contemporary Hawaiian quilts will become primarily wallhangings, rather than bed covers, and that they will continue to move away from abstraction to the depiction of more realism. The increased use of new and innovative materials, methods and procedures will continue to help quilters visually present their ideas about Hawai'i.

Traditional Hawaiian quilts continue to thrive. In spite of the fact that some traditional Hawaiian quilters have been concerned about the changes contemporary Hawaiian quilters have brought, at the same time there has been attention paid to the incredible skills demonstrated by traditional Hawaiian quilters. Their work is phenomenal and is not lessened by the contemporary Hawaiian quilting at all. If anything it brings into focus just how rich a tradition that was. As Mary Cesar stated, "The traditional Hawaiian quilters are held up on a pedestal as true artists. There is prestige because their work is validated as the true Hawaiian art. They are now the true elite. After Meali'i was named by the Smithsonian as a 'living treasure', that boosted the reputation of Hawaiian quilters throughout the country."

The Hawaiian quilt is about aloha, created with love, about the giving of love from one person to another. That has not changed as the designs and methods have evolved. Still, very few are sold, mostly they're given as gifts to represent the personal relationships between friends and within the 'ohana. In spite of rapid Westernization, the importance of relationships in Hawai'i continues to dominate social life, art and quilts in the Hawaiian Islands.

UNUSUAL APPLIQUÉ CONTEMPORARY QUILT
MAUI CALLS / Kristin De Kuiper
Design inspired by painting by Walter Rapozo ("The Flowers are Opening"). Appliqué and hand quilting by Kristin De Kuiper. 53"x33"

UNUSUAL APPLIQUÉ CONTEMPORARY QUILT
STRANGER IN PARADISE / *Joan Davis*
Design, appliqué, machine quilting and
embellishment by Joan Davis. 66"x56"

UNUSUAL APPLIQUÉ CONTEMPORARY QUILT

Moonlight on the Lagoon / Polly
Pieropan Boelter
Design, hand appliqué and hand quilting by
Polly Pieropan Boelter. 43"x30"

UNUSUAL APPLIQUÉ CONTEMPORARY QUILT

Asian Anthuriums / Mary Haunani Cesar
Design, hand appliqué, machine and hand
quilting by Mary Cesar. Fabrics dyed by Stacy
Michell. 12"x60"

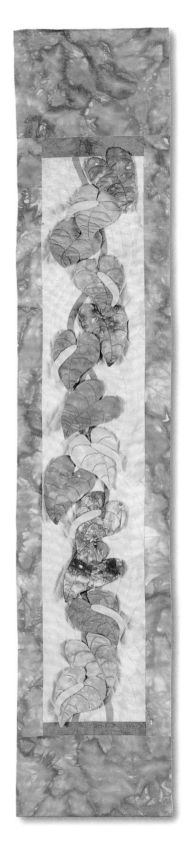

Betsy Ross Visits Maui

UNUSUAL APPLIQUÉ CONTEMPORARY QUILT
ONE IS ALL IT TAKES TO CELEBRATE /
Sue McKenna
Design, appliqué, machine and hand
quilting by Sue McKenna. 38"x48"

UNUSUAL APPLIQUÉ CONTEMPORARY QUILT
BETSY ROSS VISITS MAUI / *Kelly*
Leatherwood
Design by Natalie Barnes of Beyond the Reef.
Hand appliqué and machine quilting by Kelly
Leatherwood. 40"x40"

UNUSUAL APPLIQUÉ CONTEMPORARY QUILT
STAINED GLASS / *Sue McKenna*
Design from Glass Pattern Quarterly,
V. 16 #1, by Linda Abbot. Appliqué,
machine and hand quilting by Sue
McKenna. 29"x37"

UNUSUAL APPLIQUÉ CONTEMPORARY QUILT
*Upcountry Grace / Dianna
Grundhauser*
*Design inspired by a watercolor by
Maui artist, David Warren. Appliqué,
embellishment and machine quilting by
Dianna Grundhauser. 38"x53"*

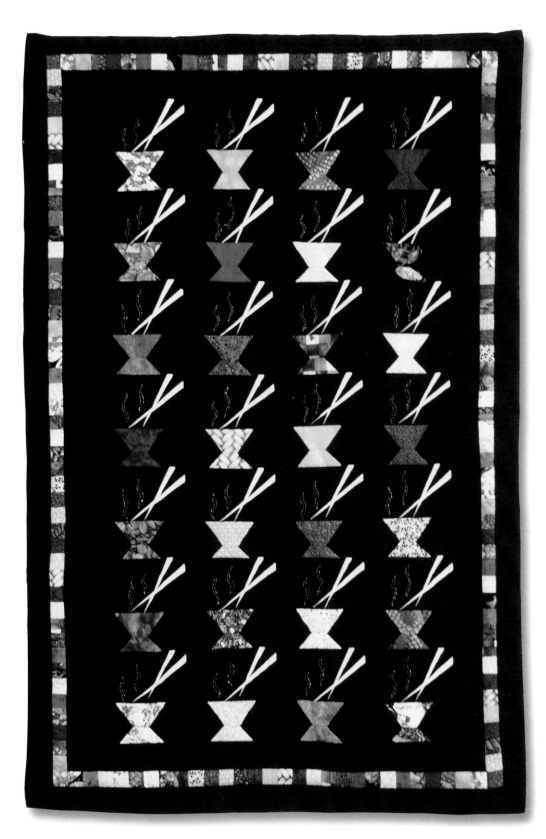

APPLIQUÉD AND PIECED
CONTEMPORARY QUILT
Two Scoop Rice /
Dianna Grundhauser
Design, piecing and
machine quilting by
Dianna Grundhauser.
2000. 48"x32"
Photograph by Paul
Kodama. Hawai'i
State Foundation on
Culture and the Arts.
3467-00.

about the author

Linda B. Arthur is Professor of Apparel Product Design and Merchandising at the University of Hawaiʻi at Manoa, and Curator of the University's Historic Costume and Textiles Collection. Dr. Arthur's teaching and publications focus on the expression of identity in dress where she explores connections between culture, ethnicity, gender, religion and dress.